Bias, Fairness & Discrimination in AI

How to Detect, Prevent & Correct Algorithmic Injustice

By Joe Correa

Published by Live Stronger Faster

This book is for educational and informational purposes only. The author and publisher are not engaged in rendering legal, financial, or other professional advice. Readers should consult a qualified professional before making any financial decisions.

First Edition

Table of Contents

Overview

Artificial intelligence is now one of the most powerful decision-making forces in human history. It decides who gets approved for a loan, who is flagged by law enforcement, who is invited to a job interview, who qualifies for healthcare, who is monitored, who is denied, and in many cases who is believed. While AI is often marketed as objective and data-driven, the reality is far more complex and far more dangerous. AI does not eliminate human bias—it industrializes it. When bias enters a machine learning system, it scales instantly, invisibly, and globally. What was once a single human prejudice becomes an automated, always-on discrimination engine capable of affecting millions of lives in seconds. This is why algorithmic bias is now one of the greatest legal, ethical, and financial risks facing governments, corporations, and society itself.

Bias in AI is not usually the result of malicious intent. It is the byproduct of flawed data, incomplete representation, historical inequality, careless design, and unexamined assumptions encoded into software. When an AI system is trained on historical data, it learns the past—not justice. If hiring data reflects decades of discrimination, the algorithm will reproduce that discrimination. If arrest data reflects over-policing of certain communities, the algorithm will predict crime where those communities live. If loan data reflects systemic exclusion, the AI will recommend denying credit to the same groups again and again. Algorithms do not know what is fair. They know what has been. And without deliberate correction, what has been becomes what will be.

This is why governments, courts, and regulators around the world are now treating biased AI systems as a form of unlawful discrimination. In many jurisdictions, companies can be sued not just for the decisions their AI makes, but for failing to prevent biased outcomes. The European Union's AI Act, U.S. civil rights law, fair lending regulations, employment law, and healthcare regulations all increasingly apply to algorithmic systems. What used to be called "a technical glitch" is now called evidence. What used to be called "a data issue" is now called discrimination. This means that bias is no longer just an ethical problem—it is a legal liability that can cost companies billions of dollars, destroy reputations, and even shut down entire product lines.

This book exists because most organizations do not understand how deeply bias is embedded in AI systems, or how dangerously exposed they already are. Many executives believe fairness is a philosophical concern. In reality, it is a compliance requirement. Many engineers believe bias is a data problem. In reality, it is a system design problem. Many policymakers believe AI discrimination is rare. In reality, it is widespread, subtle, and often invisible until damage has already been done. This book will show you where bias comes from, how it enters AI systems, how it hides inside models, and how it causes real-world harm in finance, hiring, healthcare, law enforcement, and beyond.

We begin by understanding what bias actually is. In human terms, bias means prejudice or unfair preference. In AI, bias means something more technical but no less dangerous: a systematic difference in how outcomes are produced for different groups. This can appear as higher error rates for women, minorities, or the elderly, or as lower approval rates for certain neighborhoods, accents, or education levels. Bias does not require hateful intent. It requires only imbalanced data, careless metrics, or a model trained to optimize profit instead of fairness. And once it is embedded, it becomes self-reinforcing. The system makes biased decisions, those decisions generate new data, and that data then retrains the system to become even more biased over time.

One of the most alarming features of algorithmic bias is that it often looks like accuracy. A model can be highly accurate overall while being wildly unfair to specific groups. For example, a facial recognition system may correctly identify 98 percent of white men but only 70 percent of Black women. To the company selling the product, it looks like a success. To the people being misidentified, it is a civil rights violation. This is why fairness cannot be measured only by overall performance. It must be measured across protected groups, sensitive attributes, and real-world consequences. If fairness is not explicitly tested, it will not exist.

The financial sector provides one of the clearest examples of how dangerous biased AI can be. Credit scoring algorithms, mortgage underwriting models, fraud detection systems, and lending platforms increasingly rely on machine learning to decide who receives capital. But if those systems learn from biased historical data, they will deny opportunity to the same populations that were excluded in the past. This can violate fair lending laws, anti-discrimination statutes, and consumer protection regulations. More importantly, it can trap entire communities in cycles of poverty by automating financial exclusion. A biased credit algorithm can quietly do more harm than thousands of human loan officers ever could.

Healthcare presents another high-risk environment for algorithmic bias. AI systems are now used to predict who will get sick, who should receive treatment, who gets hospital resources, and who qualifies for care. If those systems are trained on incomplete or skewed data, they can underdiagnose minorities, under-treat women, and misinterpret symptoms across different populations. In one famous case, an algorithm designed to allocate healthcare resources systematically gave less care to Black patients because it used healthcare spending as a proxy for illness, ignoring the fact that Black patients historically receive less care. The algorithm was not racist—but the data it learned from was. The result was automated discrimination.

Hiring algorithms have created another legal minefield. Many companies use AI to screen resumes, rank candidates, analyze video interviews, and predict employee success. But if those systems are trained on a workforce that is not diverse, they will learn to prefer candidates who look, speak, and behave like those already hired. This can lead to gender discrimination, racial discrimination, age discrimination, and disability discrimination at massive scale. Unlike a human recruiter, an algorithm can reject tens of thousands of people instantly, leaving a trail of digital evidence behind. When regulators or lawyers come knocking, the data will tell the story. This is why bias in AI is now one of the biggest compliance and litigation risks in technology. Regulators do not care whether a company "meant" to discriminate. They care whether it happened. And because AI systems leave logs, models, and training data, companies can no longer hide behind ignorance. If your algorithm produces discriminatory outcomes, you are responsible—even if you didn't understand how the system worked. In this new legal environment, ignorance is not a defense. Governance is.

This book will teach you how to detect bias before it becomes a lawsuit, how to audit models for fairness, how to use metrics that go beyond accuracy, and how to design systems that respect human rights while still delivering performance. You will learn about bias audits, fairness metrics, disparate impact testing, model validation, and ethical AI design principles that regulators increasingly expect organizations to follow. You will also see real-world failures—facial recognition errors, discriminatory hiring systems, biased credit models, and healthcare disasters—so you understand what happens when these principles are ignored.

Most importantly, this book will show you that fairness is not the enemy of innovation. It is the foundation of trust. In a world where algorithms decide so much of our lives, people must believe those systems are not rigged against them. Businesses that build fair AI will win customers, avoid lawsuits, attract investors, and survive regulation. Those that do not will face fines, bans, and public backlash that no amount of technology can fix.

Bias is not a bug. It is a design choice—whether intentional or not. This book gives you the tools to choose differently.

Chapter 1

Where Bias Comes From

Bias in artificial intelligence does not emerge spontaneously inside a machine. It is always inherited, transferred, or created by human systems, human data, and human decisions. Every algorithm is trained on a version of the past, and the past is not neutral. History reflects inequality in education, employment, housing, healthcare, criminal justice, and wealth. When that history becomes training data, the algorithm learns not what is right, but what was common. This is the first and most important truth about AI bias: it is not primarily a technical failure, it is a social memory problem. The model absorbs the patterns of human behavior, and if those patterns contain discrimination, exclusion, or imbalance, the AI will repeat them with mathematical confidence.

Most modern AI systems are trained using massive datasets collected from the real world. These include job applications, financial records, criminal databases, medical files, social media activity, and consumer behavior. On the surface, this data appears objective, but in reality it reflects decades or centuries of structural inequality. If women were underrepresented in leadership roles, the data will reflect that. If certain neighborhoods were over-policed, the data will show higher arrest rates there. If minorities had less access to loans, the credit data will reflect higher default rates. The algorithm does not know why these patterns exist. It only knows that they do. As a result, it may conclude that women are less suited for leadership, that certain neighborhoods are more criminal, or that certain populations are riskier borrowers, even when those conclusions are false or unjust.

Another major source of bias comes from data collection itself. What is measured, how it is measured, and who is included in a dataset all influence the outcome of an AI system. If a facial recognition dataset contains mostly light-skinned faces, the model will perform worse on darker-skinned faces. If a speech recognition dataset contains mostly male voices, the system will struggle to understand women. If a healthcare dataset contains mostly patients from wealthy hospitals, the model will not generalize to poorer communities. These are not abstract problems. They directly affect accuracy, safety, and fairness in real-world deployments.

Bias also enters AI through labeling and annotation. Many datasets rely on humans to tag images, classify text, or assign categories. These humans bring their own cultural assumptions, stereotypes, and misunderstandings into the process. A crowdworker labeling photos might misidentify people from unfamiliar cultures. A reviewer classifying emotional tone might misinterpret language patterns. A hiring dataset labeled by recruiters may reflect unconscious preferences for certain names, schools, or speech styles. When those labels become training data, the algorithm learns the biases of the people who created them.

Even when data is balanced, bias can be introduced by how a model is designed and optimized. AI systems are usually trained to maximize a specific objective, such as accuracy, profit, or efficiency.

But these objectives often conflict with fairness. A credit model optimized to maximize repayment may favor wealthier applicants. A hiring model optimized to maximize performance may favor groups that historically had more access to opportunity. A policing model optimized to predict crime may target communities that are already heavily surveilled. Without fairness constraints, the model will choose outcomes that reinforce inequality because those outcomes appear statistically optimal.

Feature selection is another powerful source of hidden bias. AI systems do not always use protected attributes like race or gender explicitly, but they often use proxies. Zip code can act as a proxy for race. Shopping habits can act as a proxy for income. Social networks can act as a proxy for culture or ethnicity. Even if a company removes race from a dataset, the algorithm may still infer it indirectly. This makes discrimination harder to detect and easier to deny, while still producing biased outcomes.

Feedback loops make bias even worse over time. When an AI system makes decisions, those decisions generate new data that feeds back into the system. If a predictive policing system sends more officers to certain neighborhoods, more crimes will be recorded there, reinforcing the model's belief that those neighborhoods are dangerous. If a loan algorithm denies credit to certain groups, it will never collect data on how well those people would have repaid. The system becomes increasingly confident in its own biased assumptions because it never sees contradictory evidence.

Organizational culture also plays a major role in where bias comes from. Many technology teams lack diversity, especially at senior levels. When the people designing AI systems all come from similar backgrounds, they are less likely to notice problems that affect others. They may not test how a system treats women, minorities, immigrants, or people with disabilities because those experiences are not part of their own lives. Bias is often invisible to those who are not harmed by it.

Finally, bias is amplified by scale. A human making a biased decision affects one person at a time. An algorithm makes millions of decisions instantly. This means that even small biases can have massive social impact. A one percent difference in error rates can translate into thousands of wrongful arrests, denied loans, or rejected job applications. What feels minor in a lab becomes devastating in the real world.

Understanding where bias comes from is the first step to controlling it. Bias does not live inside the machine. It lives in the data, the design, the goals, and the society that built the system. Until those sources are addressed, no amount of technical sophistication can make AI fair.

"The Invisible Filter"

When Maya first saw the rejection notice, she assumed it was a mistake. She had applied for a senior data analyst role at a major financial technology company, one that prided itself on innovation and fairness. Her résumé was strong, her experience deep, and her qualifications a near-perfect match. Yet within minutes of submitting her application, she received an automated email thanking her for her interest and informing her that she was not selected to proceed. There was no explanation, no feedback, and no human contact. Just a polite digital door closing in her face.

Maya had spent years working in data science. She knew what algorithms could do, and she also knew what they could get wrong. Something about the speed of the rejection felt wrong. Human recruiters usually took days or weeks. This was instant. She suspected an AI screening system had filtered her out before a person ever saw her name. Curious and unsettled, she began to investigate. Through a former colleague inside the company, she learned that an automated hiring platform ranked candidates based on patterns learned from past employees. The model looked at education, work history, language patterns, and dozens of subtle signals that humans barely noticed.

What Maya did not know was that the company's historical workforce was overwhelmingly male and came from a small group of elite universities. The algorithm had learned that those profiles correlated with "success." It had also learned, indirectly, that people who took career breaks, attended regional schools, or wrote resumes in a different tone were less likely to be hired. Maya, who had taken time off to care for a sick parent and had built her career outside the traditional corporate pipeline, did not match the algorithm's invisible template of an ideal employee.

Across town, another system was making decisions just as quietly. A small business owner named Carlos was applying for a loan to expand his grocery store. His neighborhood had been underinvested for decades, and many residents had been denied credit in the past. The bank's AI-driven risk model saw his zip code, spending patterns, and transaction history and assigned him a high-risk score. It did not see his loyal customers, his careful budgeting, or his determination. To the algorithm, he was just another data point in a historically disadvantaged area. His loan was denied in seconds.

Neither Maya nor Carlos ever saw the real reasons behind their rejection. To them, the system was a black box. But behind that box were thousands of biased data points, millions of calculations, and a set of assumptions frozen into code. The system was not angry. It was not cruel. It was simply doing what it had learned to do—repeat the past.

Maya eventually found a way to test the hiring model. Using her skills, she created simulated resumes with identical qualifications but different names, career paths, and language styles. The results were clear. Certain profiles were consistently ranked lower, even though they were just as qualified. The bias was subtle but undeniable. It was not one line of code. It was the sum of thousands of tiny statistical preferences that added up to systemic exclusion.

When she confronted the company, the executives were shocked. They had believed their AI was objective. They had trusted the numbers. But the numbers were telling a story written by history, not fairness. The company had never asked the algorithm to be just.

It had only asked it to be efficient. For Carlos, the consequences were more personal. Without the loan, he had to delay his expansion. He hired fewer employees. His store remained small, even though demand was growing. The algorithm had not just denied him money. It had denied his community opportunity. And because the system would never see the success he might have had, it would continue to believe it made the right choice.

In the end, Maya helped push the company to audit its model, rebalance its data, and introduce fairness constraints. It took time, money, and humility. But slowly, the invisible filter began to change. Different resumes started to surface. Different faces appeared in interview rooms. The system did not become perfect, but it became better.

The invisible filter had always been there, shaping lives without being seen. Now, for the first time, someone had looked inside.

Chapter 2

Training Data Risks

Training data is the raw material from which every artificial intelligence system is built. No matter how advanced an algorithm may be, it cannot transcend the quality, balance, and integrity of the data that shapes it. If the data is incomplete, skewed, outdated, or contaminated with human prejudice, the resulting AI will be too. Training data is therefore not a technical detail—it is the moral and legal foundation of every algorithmic decision. In high-stakes systems such as finance, hiring, healthcare, and law enforcement, poor training data is not just an engineering failure, it is a direct path to discrimination, liability, and social harm.

One of the most dangerous risks in training data is historical distortion. Most large datasets are collected from real-world records, which reflect decades of unequal treatment across race, gender, income, geography, and access to opportunity. These records capture what happened, not what should have happened. When an AI system learns from this data, it learns that inequality is normal. For example, if fewer women were promoted in the past, a hiring algorithm will learn that women are less likely to be successful candidates. If certain neighborhoods had higher arrest rates due to over-policing, a predictive model will treat those communities as inherently criminal. These distortions become embedded as statistical truths inside the model. Another major risk is representation imbalance. Many datasets contain far more examples from some groups than others. A facial recognition system trained mostly on lighter-skinned faces will struggle to recognize darker-skinned individuals. A voice assistant trained primarily on male voices will misinterpret women. A medical AI trained on data from urban hospitals will fail rural patients. When groups are underrepresented, the model becomes less accurate for them, and that inaccuracy becomes a form of discrimination. In safety-critical environments, this can lead to misdiagnosis, wrongful suspicion, or denied services.

Labeling errors create another hidden layer of risk. Training data often relies on humans to label examples: what is a "fraudulent" transaction, what is a "successful" employee, what is a "dangerous" person. These labels are not neutral. They reflect human judgment, cultural norms, and institutional bias. If a police department historically labeled certain behaviors as suspicious in specific communities, the AI will inherit that definition. If hiring managers labeled candidates based on subjective impressions, the model will learn those preferences. The algorithm does not know that the labels are flawed—it treats them as ground truth.

Data leakage and proxy variables further complicate the picture. Even when sensitive attributes like race or gender are removed, models often learn them indirectly through correlated data. Zip codes, education history, purchasing behavior, and social networks can all act as stand-ins for protected traits. This means that a system can discriminate without ever explicitly seeing the category it is discriminating against. This makes biased outcomes harder to detect and harder to defend in court, because the discrimination is statistical rather than explicit.

Outdated data is another serious risk. Societies change faster than datasets. A model trained on data from five years ago may no longer reflect current demographics, behaviors, or risks. If a credit model still reflects post-recession lending patterns, it may unfairly penalize groups that have since recovered. If a healthcare model is trained on older treatment protocols, it may give inaccurate recommendations. When outdated data drives decisions, people are judged by a past that no longer applies to them.

Synthetic data and data augmentation introduce their own risks when not handled carefully. While these techniques are often used to balance datasets, they can also amplify existing biases if the original data is flawed. If synthetic faces are generated based on biased training sets, the artificial data will replicate those same distortions. Instead of correcting inequality, the system multiplies it.

Data sourcing is also a major ethical and legal concern. Many organizations purchase or scrape data without fully understanding where it came from, how it was collected, or whether consent was obtained. Data gathered from surveillance, social media, or unregulated sources may violate privacy laws and human rights. When that data is used to train AI, the system becomes legally and ethically compromised from the start. A model built on unlawfully collected data is itself unlawful.

Ultimately, training data defines the boundaries of what an AI system can see, know, and judge. It determines who is visible and who is invisible, who is understood and who is misread. In the age of automated decision-making, data is destiny. Without rigorous data governance, bias audits, and continuous monitoring, even well-intentioned AI systems will drift toward discrimination. Fairness cannot be added after the fact. It must be built into the data from the very beginning.

"The Dataset That Decided"

When the city unveiled its new AI-powered public safety platform, officials promised it would make neighborhoods safer and policing fairer. The system analyzed crime reports, 911 calls, and historical arrest data to predict where officers should be deployed. It was supposed to remove human prejudice from the equation. But within months, residents of East Harbor began to notice something strange. Patrol cars were everywhere, while other parts of the city seemed untouched.

Lena, a community organizer, started collecting stories. People were being stopped more often. Minor infractions were turning into arrests. Meanwhile, similar behavior in wealthier neighborhoods went unnoticed. The city insisted the AI was neutral. It was just following the data. But Lena understood something they did not. Data is not neutral. It is a record of how power has been used.

East Harbor had been heavily policed for decades. More officers meant more stops, more searches, and more arrests. Those arrests went into the database. When the AI was trained, it saw East Harbor as a hotspot of crime. So it sent more officers there. Those officers made more arrests, which fed more data back into the system. The loop tightened, and the neighborhood became trapped inside a digital echo chamber of suspicion.

One night, Lena watched as her teenage neighbor was questioned for walking home too late. He had done nothing wrong, but his presence fit a pattern the algorithm had learned. The system did not know him. It knew only a statistical shadow of his neighborhood. That shadow was enough to trigger attention.

Lena filed public records requests and obtained the training data. It was years old, drawn from a time when the city's policing practices were far more aggressive in certain communities. The AI had inherited those practices as if they were facts about reality. The past was judging the present.

When Lena presented her findings to the city council, the room fell silent. The numbers were clear. The system was not predicting crime. It was predicting where police had historically looked for it. The algorithm had been trained to confuse enforcement with danger.

The city eventually paused the program and began rebuilding it with new data, oversight, and fairness checks. It was expensive and politically difficult. But the alternative was worse: a future where inequality was enforced by code.

The dataset had decided who was watched and who was trusted. And once people saw that truth, they could no longer pretend the machine was innocent.

Chapter 3

Facial Recognition Failures

Facial recognition technology has become one of the most widely deployed and most controversial forms of artificial intelligence in the world. Governments use it to identify suspects, verify travelers, and monitor public spaces. Companies use it to unlock phones, verify customers, and prevent fraud. Yet despite its rapid adoption, facial recognition remains one of the most biased and error-prone AI systems ever deployed at scale. Its failures are not random. They disproportionately harm women, people of color, immigrants, and young people, turning what should be a neutral security tool into a powerful engine of discrimination.

At the core of facial recognition bias lies a fundamental data problem. Most facial recognition models are trained on large image datasets scraped from the internet, surveillance cameras, and photo archives. These datasets are rarely balanced. They often contain far more images of light-skinned individuals than dark-skinned individuals, more men than women, and more adults than children or elderly people. As a result, the models become highly accurate for some groups and dangerously inaccurate for others. In controlled studies, facial recognition systems have been shown to misidentify Black women at rates many times higher than white men. When these systems are used in law enforcement or border control, those errors translate directly into wrongful suspicion, false arrests, and violations of civil rights.

Lighting, camera quality, and environmental conditions further amplify these disparities. Darker skin reflects less light, making features harder to detect in poorly lit images. Surveillance cameras, which are often low-resolution and poorly positioned, produce images that are especially challenging for accurate recognition. When these technical limitations combine with biased training data, the result is a system that works well for some faces and fails catastrophically for others. The technology does not merely make mistakes—it makes predictable mistakes that align with social inequality.

One of the most dangerous uses of facial recognition is in criminal investigations. Police departments increasingly rely on AI systems to scan mugshot databases and surveillance footage to identify potential suspects. These systems produce a list of possible matches, which officers then investigate. But when the algorithm is biased, innocent people are far more likely to be included in those lists. A false match may lead to an arrest, an interrogation, or even a prosecution. Even if the mistake is eventually corrected, the harm to the individual's reputation, mental health, and legal standing can be permanent.

Facial recognition also raises serious concerns about due process and accountability. When a human witness misidentifies someone, their testimony can be questioned, cross-examined, and evaluated. When an algorithm produces a match, it often comes with an aura of scientific authority. Judges, juries, and police officers may assume the system is objective and reliable, even when it is not. The internal workings of these models are usually opaque, making it difficult for defendants to challenge the evidence against them. This creates a dangerous imbalance of power between individuals and the institutions that use AI against them.

Beyond law enforcement, facial recognition is increasingly used in everyday life. Airports use it to verify travelers. Banks use it to confirm identity. Schools use it to monitor attendance. Retailers use it to detect shoplifters. In each of these contexts, biased errors can lead to denial of service, increased surveillance, or unfair treatment. A system that cannot accurately recognize certain faces effectively tells those people that they do not belong.

Privacy and consent issues compound these risks. Many facial recognition datasets were built without the knowledge or permission of the people whose images were included. Photos were scraped from social media, websites, and public cameras and turned into training data. Individuals never agreed to become part of an algorithmic surveillance system, yet their faces are now embedded in the technology. This raises profound questions about ownership, consent, and human dignity.

Governments and regulators are beginning to respond. Some cities have banned or restricted the use of facial recognition by police. The European Union has proposed strict limits on biometric surveillance. Courts are increasingly skeptical of algorithmic evidence. But the technology continues to spread, driven by powerful commercial and security interests. Without strong governance, the same biased systems will be deployed again and again, causing harm on a massive scale.

Facial recognition failures are not a side effect of immature technology. They are the result of choices about data, design, and deployment. When companies and governments prioritize speed, convenience, or profit over fairness and accuracy, people pay the price. If this technology is to be used at all, it must be subjected to rigorous testing, transparency, and oversight. Otherwise, it will remain a digital mirror of society's deepest inequalities.

"The Wrong Face"

The first time Marcus heard his name spoken by a police officer, he thought it was a joke. He had just finished a late shift at the warehouse and was walking home when a patrol car pulled up beside him. The officer stepped out, looked at a tablet, and said, "Marcus Reed?" Marcus nodded, confused. Within seconds, he was in handcuffs.

At the station, they showed him a grainy still image from a security camera. It was blurry and poorly lit, but the AI system had matched it to his driver's license photo. The system said there was a high probability it was him. Marcus tried to explain that he had never been near the place where the crime happened. It did not matter. The machine had spoken.

It took days for a public defender to get access to the evidence. By then, Marcus had missed work, frightened his family, and been labeled a suspect in a crime he did not commit. When the lawyer finally looked at the image, she immediately saw the problem. The face in the photo barely resembled Marcus. But the algorithm had been trained on a database that struggled to distinguish between people with similar skin tones and facial structures. To the system, Marcus was close enough.

The charges were eventually dropped, but the damage was done. His employer was wary. His neighbors whispered. Marcus felt like his identity had been taken from him and replaced with a probability score.

He later learned that dozens of others had been falsely flagged by the same system. They all shared one thing in common: the algorithm could not see them clearly. In a world run by machines, being misseen was enough to change a life forever.

Chapter 4

Hiring Algorithms Gone Wrong

Hiring is one of the most powerful gatekeeping functions in society. It determines who gains access to income, stability, healthcare, social mobility, and opportunity. When artificial intelligence enters this process, it does not merely speed up recruitment—it reshapes who is allowed to participate in the economy. Hiring algorithms now screen résumés, analyze video interviews, rank candidates, and predict future job performance. While these tools are often promoted as neutral and efficient, they have become some of the most dangerous sources of algorithmic discrimination in modern business.

The fundamental problem with AI hiring systems is that they are trained on past hiring data, and past hiring data is deeply biased. Most companies have historically favored certain schools, certain career paths, certain speech patterns, and certain demographic groups. If a company's workforce was mostly male, mostly white, or mostly from elite institutions, the algorithm will learn that those characteristics correlate with success. It will then prefer candidates who look like the people who were hired before. This creates a digital version of old-boy networks, where similarity is mistaken for merit.

Resume screening algorithms often rely on keyword matching, career trajectory analysis, and statistical patterns. Thesc tools may reject highly capable candidates simply because their experience does not follow a conventional path. Women who took time off for caregiving, immigrants who attended foreign universities, veterans who served instead of working in corporate roles, and self-taught technologists can all be filtered out before a human ever sees their application. The algorithm does not understand context. It only sees deviation from the pattern it was trained to value.

Video interview analysis introduces even more troubling risks. Some AI systems claim to evaluate facial expressions, voice tone, eye movement, and body language to predict traits like confidence, honesty, or leadership. These systems are built on pseudoscientific assumptions and culturally biased data. What looks like confidence in one culture may look like arrogance or disrespect in another. What looks like nervousness in one person may be a disability, a language barrier, or a trauma response. When these signals are reduced to numerical scores, people are judged not by their ability to do the job, but by how well they fit an algorithm's narrow definition of "normal."

Disability discrimination is especially common in AI-driven hiring. Neurodivergent individuals, people with speech impairments, hearing loss, or physical differences can be unfairly penalized by systems that expect certain patterns of movement or communication. Because these tools are often marketed as objective, employers may not even realize they are excluding qualified candidates. Yet under disability law in many countries, using a system that disproportionately harms people with disabilities can be illegal, even if the discrimination is unintentional.

Another major issue is transparency. Most hiring algorithms are proprietary, meaning companies cannot fully explain how candidates are evaluated. When a rejected applicant asks why they were not selected, the employer may have no meaningful answer. This creates a legal and ethical crisis. Anti-discrimination laws require that hiring decisions be explainable and justifiable. An algorithm that cannot explain itself puts the employer at serious risk.

Bias in hiring algorithms also creates long-term feedback loops. If the system selects candidates from a narrow demographic, the workforce becomes less diverse. That new workforce generates new data, which is then used to retrain the algorithm. Over time, the model becomes even more biased because it has never seen successful employees from excluded groups. The system becomes a closed loop of exclusion, reinforcing inequality while appearing mathematically sound.

From a business perspective, this is not just an ethical failure—it is a strategic one. Companies that use biased hiring systems lose access to vast pools of talent. They become less innovative, less adaptable, and less competitive. They also expose themselves to lawsuits, regulatory penalties, and reputational damage. In a world where diversity and inclusion are increasingly demanded by employees, customers, and investors, algorithmic discrimination is a ticking time bomb.

Fair hiring requires more than simply installing AI. It requires careful data curation, bias testing, human oversight, and a commitment to equal opportunity. Algorithms must be designed to expand access, not narrow it. Otherwise, the future of work will be controlled not by human potential, but by the blind patterns of the past.

"The Resume That Never Reached a Human"

Nina had applied to over a hundred jobs in the past six months. Each time, she customized her résumé, wrote thoughtful cover letters, and waited. Each time, the response was the same: a polite rejection email, often arriving within hours. She knew she was qualified. She had years of experience, strong references, and a deep passion for her field. Yet it felt as if no one was ever truly reading her application.

One evening, frustrated and exhausted, Nina reached out to a former coworker who now worked in HR at a large corporation. He explained what was really happening. Most applications, he said, were screened by an AI system before any recruiter saw them. The algorithm ranked candidates based on patterns learned from past hires. Those who scored too low were automatically rejected.

Nina realized the truth with a sinking feeling. Her career path had been unconventional. She had taken time off to care for her mother. She had worked for small nonprofits instead of big brands. She had taught herself new skills instead of earning expensive certifications.

To a human, her story showed resilience and adaptability. To an algorithm, it looked like deviation.

When her friend tested her résumé against the system, the result was clear. The AI flagged her as a low match, not because she lacked ability, but because she did not resemble the people who had been hired before. Her future was being judged by the past of a company she had never even met. Nina eventually found a firm that valued human review and diversity. But she never forgot how easily she had been erased by a machine. Somewhere in a server, her résumé still sat, rejected by an invisible gatekeeper that never knew her name, her effort, or her worth.

Chapter 5

Credit & Lending Discrimination

Artificial intelligence has become the invisible engine behind modern credit decisions. From credit cards and mortgages to small-business loans, auto financing, and insurance underwriting, AI systems now determine who gets approved, how much they can borrow, and at what price. These systems promise speed, efficiency, and objectivity, but they also carry extraordinary power over people's financial lives. When bias enters these models, it does not simply inconvenience applicants—it reshapes who can build wealth, who can own property, who can start businesses, and who can escape poverty. In this sense, biased credit AI is not just unfair; it is economically destructive.

Historically, lending has always been one of the most discriminatory areas of society. Redlining, racial steering, unequal access to banking, and predatory lending have shaped entire communities for generations. When AI models are trained on historical loan performance data, they inherit this legacy. The system learns patterns that reflect unequal access to opportunity rather than actual creditworthiness. A borrower from a marginalized neighborhood may appear riskier simply because people in that area were denied good loans in the past, forcing them into worse financial situations. The model sees higher default rates and treats them as personal risk, even though they are the result of structural exclusion.

One of the most dangerous aspects of AI-driven credit scoring is the use of proxy variables. Even if a model does not explicitly include race, gender, or ethnicity, it can still infer those traits through data such as zip code, shopping behavior, device type, language patterns, or social connections. These variables act as silent stand-ins for protected classes. The result is a system that can discriminate without appearing to do so. From a legal perspective, this is especially dangerous because regulators care about outcomes, not just intent. If a model produces disparate impacts, the lender can still be held liable.

Another serious risk comes from alternative data sources. Many modern credit models use social media activity, online behavior, transaction histories, and even smartphone data to assess borrowers. While these sources may improve prediction in some cases, they also introduce enormous fairness risks. People with less access to technology, different cultural habits, or irregular income patterns may be unfairly penalized. Gig workers, immigrants, freelancers, and small business owners can be misclassified as high-risk simply because their financial lives do not fit a traditional template.

Feedback loops make these systems even more harmful. When an AI denies credit to a group, it prevents that group from generating positive repayment data. The system then never learns that those borrowers could have succeeded. Over time, entire populations become invisible to the model's understanding of success. The algorithm becomes increasingly confident that it is right, even as it locks people out of the economy.

Regulators around the world are now paying close attention to these risks. In the United States, fair lending laws such as the Equal Credit Opportunity Act and the Fair Housing Act apply to algorithmic decisions just as they do to human ones. In Europe, data protection and anti-discrimination laws place strict limits on automated decision-making. Financial institutions are being required to explain how their models work, demonstrate fairness, and prove that protected groups are not being harmed. This is forcing banks and fintech companies to rethink how they build and deploy AI.

The challenge is that many credit models are highly complex and opaque. Deep learning systems can use thousands of variables and nonlinear interactions that are difficult to interpret. When a borrower is denied, even the company that built the model may not fully understand why. This lack of explainability makes compliance and accountability extremely difficult. It also undermines public trust. People do not accept financial decisions that they cannot understand, especially when those decisions affect their future.

True fairness in credit AI requires more than just removing sensitive variables. It requires rethinking what risk actually means. Is risk a reflection of individual behavior, or is it a reflection of unequal opportunity? Models that fail to account for structural inequality will always confuse the two. Ethical credit AI must be designed to recognize context, not just correlations.

Ultimately, credit is one of the most powerful levers of social mobility. When AI controls that lever, it must be held to the highest standards of fairness, transparency, and accountability. Otherwise, the technology that was meant to democratize finance will instead become a new form of digital redlining.

"The Algorithm That Denied a Dream"

Jamal had spent ten years building his small construction business from nothing. He had grown up in a neighborhood where banks rarely approved loans, so he had relied on cash, personal connections, and relentless work. When a major contract finally came his way, he needed capital to buy equipment and hire workers. Confident in his track record, he applied for a business loan through a new AI-powered lending platform that promised fast, fair decisions.

The answer came in seconds: denied.

There was no explanation beyond a vague reference to risk factors. Jamal was stunned. His revenue was strong. His clients were reliable. His debts were low. Yet the system had judged him unworthy. When he called customer service, the representative could not tell him what went wrong. The decision had been made by an algorithm, and the algorithm did not speak.

What Jamal did not know was that the model had been trained on years of small-business loan data that reflected decades of unequal access to capital. Businesses in his neighborhood had historically received fewer loans and paid higher interest rates. Many had struggled because they were underfunded from the start. The AI saw this pattern and concluded that Jamal's zip code meant higher risk.

The system also analyzed his transaction history. Because many of his customers paid in cash or through informal channels, his financial profile looked less stable than a company that dealt only with large corporations. The algorithm did not understand community economics. It only understood patterns.

Without the loan, Jamal lost the contract. He laid off workers. A chance to grow into a regional company disappeared. The AI had not just denied him money. It had denied his future.

Months later, a journalist uncovered widespread bias in the lending platform. Regulators stepped in. The company apologized and promised reforms. But for Jamal, the moment had passed.

Somewhere in a database, his application still existed, marked as a risk. A line of code had decided that his dream was too dangerous to fund.

Chapter 6

Healthcare Bias

Healthcare is one of the most ethically sensitive domains in which artificial intelligence is now deeply embedded. AI systems are used to predict disease risk, allocate hospital resources, recommend treatments, prioritize patients, and even determine who qualifies for life-saving interventions. When these systems are fair and accurate, they can dramatically improve medical outcomes. When they are biased, they can quietly decide who lives longer, who receives care, and who is left behind. Healthcare bias in AI is therefore not just a technical or legal issue—it is a matter of life and death.

Most medical AI systems are trained on historical patient data, including diagnoses, treatments, costs, and outcomes. This data reflects how healthcare has been delivered, not how it should have been delivered. For decades, women, racial minorities, disabled individuals, and low-income patients have received less testing, fewer referrals, and lower-quality care. When AI learns from this data, it internalizes those disparities as if they were medical truths. A model might learn that women are less likely to have heart disease because they were underdiagnosed. It might learn that certain racial groups need fewer medical resources because they historically received less. The algorithm does not understand injustice—it interprets injustice as evidence.

One of the most damaging forms of healthcare bias comes from the use of proxy variables. Many AI systems use healthcare spending, frequency of doctor visits, or insurance claims as indicators of patient need. But spending is not the same as illness. Wealthier patients have more access to care, more diagnostic tests, and more expensive treatments. Poorer patients often delay care, receive fewer interventions, and generate lower costs even when they are just as sick. When an AI uses spending as a proxy for severity, it will systematically underestimate the needs of marginalized patients and overestimate the needs of wealthier ones.

Another serious risk comes from underrepresentation in clinical data. Many medical datasets are built from research hospitals, academic centers, and clinical trials that do not reflect the full diversity of the population. Minority groups, rural patients, pregnant women, and the elderly are often underrepresented. As a result, AI models trained on these datasets may perform well for some patients and dangerously poorly for others. A diagnostic tool might miss cancer in one group, misclassify symptoms in another, or recommend inappropriate treatments for people who were not well represented in the training data.

Bias can also arise from how diseases are defined and labeled. Medical diagnoses are not purely objective; they are influenced by physician judgment, institutional practices, and cultural assumptions. If certain groups are more likely to be labeled as non-compliant, anxious, or drug-seeking, those labels will appear in the data. The AI will then learn to associate those groups with lower priority or lower quality care. The system does not see people—it sees categories that were shaped by human prejudice.

The consequences of biased healthcare AI are often invisible because they are embedded in complex systems. A patient may never know that an algorithm downgraded their risk score or deprioritized them for treatment. A doctor may trust the system's recommendation without realizing it is flawed. Hospitals may allocate resources based on AI outputs that quietly favor some populations over others. The harm accumulates slowly, quietly, and across millions of decisions.

From a legal and regulatory perspective, healthcare AI bias is becoming a major concern. Laws protecting patients from discrimination, such as civil rights statutes and disability protections, apply to algorithmic decisions just as they do to human ones. Medical device regulators are also beginning to treat AI systems as high-risk technologies that require rigorous validation and oversight. Hospitals and vendors that deploy biased systems may face lawsuits, regulatory penalties, and loss of public trust.

Ethical healthcare AI requires more than technical accuracy. It requires deliberate efforts to balance datasets, test performance across demographic groups, audit outcomes, and involve diverse experts in system design. It also requires transparency so that doctors and patients can understand how decisions are being made. Without these safeguards, AI will not eliminate inequality in medicine—it will encode it into software.

Healthcare should be guided by compassion, science, and respect for human dignity. When algorithms replace or influence medical judgment, they must be held to those same values. Otherwise, the future of medicine will be one in which data decides who deserves to be healed.

"The Score That Almost Killed Her"

Aisha had always trusted doctors. When she felt a sharp pain in her chest and shortness of breath, she went straight to the emergency room. The hospital had recently implemented a new AI-driven triage system that ranked patients by risk and urgency. As soon as Aisha was checked in, the system analyzed her symptoms, medical history, and insurance data and produced a score. The screen showed green. Low risk.

She waited.

Minutes turned into hours. Other patients were seen first. Aisha's pain worsened, but the nurses kept glancing at the screen. The algorithm said she was stable. What it did not know was that women, especially women of color, are often underdiagnosed when it comes to heart conditions. Their symptoms do not always match the patterns in the data.

Aisha collapsed in the waiting room. Only then did a doctor intervene. Tests revealed she was having a heart attack.

Later, a hospital review uncovered the truth. The AI system had been trained on years of data in which patients like Aisha had received less aggressive treatment. It used healthcare spending as a proxy for risk. Because she had fewer past claims and lower medical costs, the system assumed she was healthier than she was.

The algorithm had not intended to harm her. But it had learned from a system that had.

Aisha survived, but she never forgot how close she came to dying because a machine had misjudged her worth. In a hospital full of technology, her life had been reduced to a number—and that number was wrong.

Chapter 7

Legal Liability for Bias

As artificial intelligence becomes embedded in the core decision-making systems of modern organizations, the legal system is rapidly adapting to treat biased algorithms as a form of unlawful discrimination. What once appeared to be a technical matter of software performance has now become a serious issue of civil rights, consumer protection, employment law, financial regulation, and corporate accountability. Companies that deploy biased AI systems are discovering that they cannot hide behind automation. In the eyes of the law, an algorithm is an extension of the organization that uses it. If it discriminates, the organization discriminates.

Historically, discrimination law focused on human intent. Courts looked for evidence that a person meant to treat others unfairly. But modern law increasingly focuses on outcomes. If a hiring system produces disproportionately negative results for women or minorities, that is evidence of discrimination, even if no one intended it. The same applies to credit decisions, insurance pricing, housing approvals, healthcare access, and public services. When an AI system produces biased outcomes, regulators and courts treat it as if a human decision-maker had done so. The fact that a computer made the decision does not reduce liability—it often increases it, because automated systems operate at scale.

In the financial sector, lenders that use AI-driven underwriting systems are subject to fair lending laws that prohibit disparate impact. This means that even if a model does not explicitly consider race, it can still be illegal if its results disproportionately harm protected groups. Regulators can demand documentation, audit models, and require changes to algorithms. Banks have already faced enforcement actions for models that produced biased credit outcomes, and these cases are expected to increase as AI becomes more prevalent.

Employment law is another major area of exposure. Companies that use AI to screen resumes, analyze video interviews, or rank candidates must comply with anti-discrimination statutes. If an algorithm systematically rejects older workers, women, people with disabilities, or racial minorities, the employer can be sued. Because these systems generate detailed logs and records, plaintiffs' lawyers can use the company's own data to prove bias. What was once invisible in human hiring is now measurable in code.

Healthcare and insurance bring additional layers of liability. Biased AI systems that deny or delay care can violate civil rights laws, disability protections, and patient safety regulations. Insurance models that charge higher rates to certain groups can violate anti-discrimination and consumer protection laws. In these fields, harm is not just financial–it is physical and emotional, which increases the potential damages in lawsuits.

Data protection and privacy laws also intersect with algorithmic bias. Regulations like the European Union's GDPR give individuals the right to understand automated decisions that affect them and to challenge those decisions. If a company cannot explain how its model works or why a person was denied a service, it may be in violation of the law. This creates a powerful incentive for organizations to adopt explainable, auditable AI rather than opaque black boxes.

One of the most important developments in this area is the rise of algorithmic audits. Regulators and courts are increasingly requiring companies to test their models for bias, document their training data, and prove that they have taken steps to mitigate discrimination. Failure to do so can be used as evidence of negligence or willful disregard. In other words, not knowing your AI is biased is no longer an excuse. You are expected to know.

From a corporate governance perspective, this means AI risk must be treated like any other major compliance risk. Boards of directors, legal teams, and executives must understand how their systems work, where bias might arise, and what safeguards are in place. Ignoring these issues can lead to regulatory fines, class-action lawsuits, loss of licenses, and irreparable reputational harm.

Legal liability is not meant to stop innovation. It is meant to ensure that innovation does not come at the expense of human rights. When AI systems decide who gets hired, who gets a loan, who receives medical care, and who is watched by the state, they must be held to the same standards of fairness and accountability as any human decision-maker. The law is making this clear: if your algorithm discriminates, you will answer for it.

"The Lawsuit That Exposed the Code"

When Rachel lost her job application, she assumed it was just bad luck. But when it happened again and again, she began to suspect something more. She was highly qualified, yet she never even reached the interview stage. A friend who worked in tech suggested she might be facing an algorithmic gatekeeper. Rachel decided to fight back.

With the help of a civil rights attorney, she filed a lawsuit against the company, demanding access to the hiring system that had rejected her. The company resisted, claiming the algorithm was proprietary. But the court ordered them to disclose it. What the lawyers found was explosive.

The model had been trained on ten years of employee data from a workforce that was overwhelmingly male. It had learned to associate leadership with masculine speech patterns, uninterrupted career paths, and certain schools. Women who had taken time off or followed different paths were scored lower, even when they were just as capable.

When the evidence was presented in court, the company's defense collapsed. The algorithm's own data showed a clear pattern of discrimination. The judge ruled that the company had violated employment law by using a system that produced biased outcomes.

The case made headlines. Other companies began auditing their models. Regulators issued new guidelines. Rachel won more than compensation—she helped change how AI would be used in hiring.

The code had spoken, and in doing so, it had confessed.

Chapter 8

Bias Audits

Bias audits are becoming one of the most critical tools in modern AI governance. As algorithms take over decisions once made by humans, organizations must be able to prove that their systems operate fairly, lawfully, and responsibly. A bias audit is a structured, evidence-based process for examining whether an AI system produces unequal outcomes for different groups and for identifying the causes of those disparities. Without audits, companies are effectively flying blind, deploying powerful decision engines without knowing whether they are harming people or violating the law.

At its core, a bias audit asks a simple question: does this system treat everyone equally? But answering that question is complex. AI models often use hundreds or thousands of variables, many of which interact in subtle ways. A bias audit begins by defining the protected groups that matter, such as race, gender, age, disability status, or socioeconomic background. It then examines how the system's outputs differ across those groups. Are approval rates lower for certain populations? Are error rates higher? Are some people more likely to be flagged as risky, suspicious, or unqualified?

One of the most important steps in a bias audit is outcome testing. This involves running the model on real or simulated data and measuring how its decisions vary by group. For example, a credit model might be tested to see whether equally qualified applicants receive different interest rates based on race or zip code. A hiring model might be evaluated to see whether women are ranked lower than men with similar credentials. These tests go beyond surface-level accuracy and look directly at fairness.

Data analysis is another key component. Auditors must examine the training data to see whether certain groups are underrepresented, mislabeled, or historically disadvantaged. If the data itself is biased, the model will almost certainly be biased too. This is why audits often involve rebalancing datasets, correcting labels, or introducing new data that better reflects the population the system is meant to serve.

Model inspection is also essential. Some algorithms are more prone to bias than others. Highly complex black-box models may produce accurate predictions but make it difficult to understand why decisions are made. Auditors may use explainability tools to see which variables influence outcomes and whether those variables act as proxies for protected traits. If a model is effectively using zip code to infer race or income, that must be addressed.

Bias audits are not one-time events. AI systems change over time as they are retrained on new data and deployed in new contexts. A model that was fair last year may become biased this year as demographics shift or business practices change. Continuous monitoring is therefore necessary. Leading organizations now treat bias audits as part of their regular compliance cycle, similar to financial audits or cybersecurity reviews.

From a legal standpoint, bias audits are quickly becoming a requirement rather than a best practice. Regulators increasingly expect companies to demonstrate that they have tested their systems and taken steps to prevent discrimination. Failure to conduct an audit can be seen as negligence. In court, a documented bias audit can be the difference between liability and compliance.

Perhaps most importantly, bias audits force organizations to confront uncomfortable truths about their data, their assumptions, and their values. They reveal where systems fail and where people are being treated unfairly. This can be difficult, but it is also an opportunity to build trust. Companies that take fairness seriously can differentiate themselves in a crowded market and build long-term relationships with customers and communities.

Bias audits do not eliminate all risk, but they make invisible harms visible. In a world where algorithms increasingly govern opportunity, that visibility is essential for justice.

"The Audit That Changed Everything"

When the fintech startup BrightLend launched its new AI-powered loan platform, investors were thrilled. Approval times dropped from days to seconds. Profits soared. But something was wrong. Community groups began to complain that certain neighborhoods were being denied credit at unusually high rates.

Elena, the company's compliance officer, insisted on a bias audit. The executives were reluctant. The system was working, they said.

Why slow it down? But Elena knew that what looked like success could be hiding discrimination.

The audit revealed a troubling pattern. Applicants from minority neighborhoods were far more likely to be denied, even when their financial profiles were similar to those of approved borrowers. The model was using zip code and spending behavior as proxies for race and income. No one had intended this, but the impact was real.

Elena presented the findings to the board. The room was silent. They had built a machine that was quietly repeating the injustices of the past.

Instead of burying the report, the company acted. They retrained the model, removed problematic variables, and implemented ongoing monitoring. It cost them money in the short term, but something else happened. Trust returned. Regulators took notice. Customers felt safer.

The audit had not just fixed a model. It had changed a company's soul.

Chapter 9

Fairness Metrics

Fairness in artificial intelligence cannot be achieved through good intentions alone. It must be measured, tested, monitored, and enforced using rigorous quantitative tools known as fairness metrics. These metrics allow organizations to evaluate whether an AI system treats different groups equitably and whether its decisions create unjustified disparities. Without fairness metrics, bias remains invisible. With them, discrimination becomes something that can be detected, challenged, and corrected. In the modern regulatory and ethical environment, fairness metrics are no longer optional—they are essential to lawful and responsible AI deployment.

At a basic level, fairness metrics compare how different groups are treated by a model. These groups are often defined by protected characteristics such as race, gender, age, disability, or income level. The most common question is whether the system produces significantly different outcomes for these groups when they are similarly qualified. For example, do men and women with the same experience receive the same hiring scores? Do borrowers with similar credit profiles receive the same loan terms regardless of zip code or ethnicity? These comparisons form the foundation of fairness testing.

One of the most widely used metrics is demographic parity. This measures whether different groups receive positive outcomes at similar rates. In hiring, this might mean the percentage of men and women selected. In lending, it might mean the percentage of applicants approved. While demographic parity is easy to calculate, it can be misleading. If one group has been historically excluded from opportunity, forcing equal outcomes without considering qualifications may create new forms of unfairness. For this reason, demographic parity is often used as a warning signal rather than a final verdict.

Another important metric is equalized odds. This looks at whether error rates are similar across groups. In other words, does the model make false positives and false negatives at similar rates for different populations? In facial recognition, this might mean whether misidentifications occur more often for one race than another. In credit scoring, it might mean whether good borrowers are denied more often in one group. Equalized odds focuses on fairness in mistakes, which is often where harm occurs.

Predictive parity is another key concept. It measures whether a model's predictions mean the same thing for everyone. If a risk score of 700 predicts a 10 percent default rate for one group and a 30 percent default rate for another, the system is not fair, even if overall accuracy is high. This kind of hidden disparity can lead to unequal pricing, access, and treatment.

Choosing the right fairness metrics is not straightforward because many of them conflict with one another. A system cannot always satisfy demographic parity, equalized odds, and predictive parity at the same time. Organizations must decide which trade-offs are acceptable based on the legal, ethical, and social context of the application. In criminal justice, minimizing false positives for marginalized groups may be the priority. In healthcare, equal access to treatment may matter more. In finance, avoiding discriminatory denial of credit may be paramount.

Fairness metrics must also be applied continuously. An AI system that is fair today may become biased tomorrow as data changes, user behavior shifts, or business incentives evolve. This is why leading organizations build fairness monitoring into their production systems. Dashboards track disparities in real time. Alerts signal when thresholds are crossed. Human reviewers investigate and intervene.

From a compliance perspective, fairness metrics provide evidence. Regulators and courts increasingly expect organizations to demonstrate that they have tested their systems and understand their impacts. A company that cannot show fairness metrics may be assumed to be negligent. Conversely, a company that actively measures and manages bias can demonstrate good faith and due diligence.

Fairness metrics do not make AI perfect, but they make it accountable. They turn abstract values into numbers that can be audited, debated, and improved. In a world where algorithms increasingly govern opportunity, those numbers are one of the most powerful tools we have to ensure justice.

"The Numbers That Told the Truth"

When the national education agency rolled out its AI-powered scholarship system, the goal was to make awards more objective and merit-based. Thousands of students submitted applications, and the algorithm ranked them according to grades, test scores, extracurricular activities, and predicted future success. The results looked efficient. Scholarships were awarded in minutes instead of months. But a quiet unease spread through advocacy groups who noticed something strange. Fewer students from low-income and minority backgrounds were being selected.

Dr. Lena Ortiz, a data scientist who worked for a nonprofit, requested the results under public records laws. When she began analyzing the data, the story became clear. Students from wealthier schools were being selected at much higher rates, even when their academic records were similar to those from poorer districts. The algorithm was not measuring potential. It was measuring privilege.

Lena applied fairness metrics to the model's outputs. Demographic parity showed huge gaps. Equalized odds revealed that high-performing students from marginalized backgrounds were far more likely to be rejected. Predictive parity showed that a top score did not mean the same thing for every student. The numbers told a story that the agency could not ignore.

When Lena presented her findings to lawmakers, the room was stunned. The AI had been trained on years of scholarship data that favored students from elite schools. It had learned that those backgrounds correlated with success. It had not learned about talent in underfunded classrooms.

The system was suspended, rebalanced, and rebuilt. New fairness thresholds were introduced. Human reviewers were added back into the process. It took time, but the next round of scholarships looked different. Students who had once been invisible began to appear.

For Lena, the victory was not just statistical. It was human. Behind every number was a dream. And for the first time, the numbers had spoken in their defense.

Chapter 10
Ethical AI Design

Ethical AI design is the final and most important defense against algorithmic bias, discrimination, and injustice. While audits, fairness metrics, and legal compliance help identify and limit harm after a system is built, ethical design determines whether harm is created in the first place. Ethical AI design means embedding fairness, accountability, transparency, and human dignity directly into the architecture of artificial intelligence systems. It treats ethics not as an afterthought or a compliance checkbox, but as a foundational engineering requirement.

At the heart of ethical AI design is the recognition that technology is not neutral. Every design choice reflects values. Choosing which data to collect, which features to include, which objectives to optimize, and which users to prioritize all shape how an AI system will affect people. An algorithm trained to maximize profit will behave differently from one trained to maximize social good. A model optimized for efficiency may sacrifice fairness. Ethical design requires developers to make these trade-offs consciously and to choose outcomes that respect human rights.

One of the most important principles of ethical AI design is inclusion. Systems must be built using data that reflects the full diversity of the population they will serve. This means actively seeking out underrepresented groups, correcting imbalances, and testing performance across demographic categories. Inclusion also means involving diverse voices in the design process. Engineers, ethicists, legal experts, and representatives of affected communities must all have a seat at the table. Without this, blind spots are inevitable.

Transparency is another core principle. Ethical AI systems must be explainable to the people who are affected by them. Users have the right to know how decisions are made, what data is used, and how they can challenge or appeal outcomes. This requires using interpretable models when possible, building explanation tools, and providing meaningful disclosures. A system that cannot explain itself cannot be trusted.

Human oversight is equally essential. No AI system should operate in isolation when making high-stakes decisions about people's lives. Ethical design requires human-in-the-loop processes that allow trained professionals to review, override, and correct algorithmic outputs. This ensures that context, compassion, and judgment are never fully replaced by code.

Ethical AI design also demands continuous monitoring. Even well-designed systems can drift over time as data changes and new patterns emerge. Regular testing for bias, performance, and unintended consequences is necessary to maintain fairness. This turns ethics into an ongoing responsibility rather than a one-time achievement.

From a business perspective, ethical AI is not a burden—it is a competitive advantage. Companies that build trustworthy systems earn customer loyalty, avoid legal risk, and attract top talent. Those that cut corners may gain short-term efficiency but face long-term backlash. In an era of increasing regulation and public scrutiny, ethical design is the path to sustainable innovation.

Ultimately, ethical AI design is about remembering that behind every data point is a human being. Algorithms may be powerful, but they must always serve human dignity. When fairness is built into the code, technology becomes a force for justice rather than a tool of inequality.

"The System They Chose to Build"

The city of Havenbrook had one chance to get it right. After years of controversy over biased algorithms, the mayor announced a new initiative to rebuild the city's digital infrastructure from the ground up. Every system that affected housing, employment, policing, and healthcare would be redesigned under strict ethical guidelines. The project was ambitious, expensive, and politically risky. But the old systems had failed too many people.

Mara, a young engineer, was assigned to the team building the new housing allocation AI. In the past, the system had quietly favored wealthier applicants and long-time residents, leaving immigrants, low-income families, and the disabled waiting for years. This time, things would be different. Mara insisted on starting with diverse data, fairness constraints, and transparency tools. She fought to include community advocates in design meetings. She argued for human review panels and clear appeal processes.

Not everyone agreed. Some executives wanted faster results. Some politicians wanted numbers that looked good. But Mara held her ground. She knew that every shortcut would become a scar.

When the new system launched, the results were not perfect, but they were fairer. Families who had never been considered before began receiving housing. Appeals were heard. Mistakes were corrected. People could finally see how decisions were made.

One evening, Mara visited a community center and met a woman who had just been approved for an apartment after years of homelessness. The woman did not know Mara. She did not know about fairness metrics or data governance. She only knew that a door had finally opened.

As Mara walked home, she realized something profound. Ethical AI was not about machines. It was about the lives they touched. And this time, they had chosen to build something that deserved trust.

Chapter 11

The Future of Fair AI

The future of artificial intelligence will not be decided by faster processors or larger models alone. It will be decided by whether society chooses to build systems that are fair, accountable, and worthy of trust. As AI becomes embedded in every major institution—governments, banks, hospitals, schools, employers, and courts—the stakes of fairness grow exponentially. The question is no longer whether biased AI will cause harm, but whether humanity will have the courage and wisdom to prevent that harm before it becomes irreversible.

In the coming years, fairness will become a primary design constraint for all high-impact AI systems. Just as safety standards transformed industries like aviation and pharmaceuticals, fairness standards will transform AI. Regulators will increasingly require companies to demonstrate that their systems do not produce unjustified disparities. This will push developers to adopt better data practices, more transparent models, and more rigorous testing. Fairness will become something that is engineered, not merely hoped for.

Advances in explainable AI will play a central role in this transformation. New tools are emerging that allow complex models to provide human-readable reasons for their decisions. These tools will make it easier to identify bias, correct errors, and build trust with users. When people can see why an AI made a decision, they are more likely to accept it—or challenge it when it is wrong. Transparency is the bridge between technology and accountability.

The future will also bring new forms of participatory design. Communities affected by AI systems will demand a voice in how those systems are built. This will lead to more inclusive development processes, where technologists work alongside ethicists, lawyers, and the public. AI will no longer be something done to people. It will be something built with them.

International cooperation will be another key factor. Bias does not stop at national borders, and neither does technology. Global standards for ethical AI will help prevent a race to the bottom where companies deploy harmful systems in less regulated regions. Treaties, agreements, and shared frameworks will shape how fairness is enforced worldwide.

Perhaps most importantly, the future of fair AI depends on education. Engineers must be trained to think ethically. Executives must understand their responsibilities. Citizens must know their rights. A society that understands how algorithms work is better equipped to demand justice from them.

The future is not predetermined. AI can either deepen inequality or help correct it. The choice belongs to those who design, deploy, and govern these systems. Fairness is not a limitation on innovation. It is the condition that makes innovation worth having.

"The Generation That Refused to Be Judged"

In the year 2045, AI systems made nearly every important decision in the world. They determined who got into universities, who received medical treatment, who qualified for housing, and who was flagged as a security risk. Most people had grown used to it. But a new generation was growing restless.

They called themselves the Unscored.

Unlike their parents, who had accepted algorithmic ratings as a fact of life, the Unscored refused to let machines define their worth. They demanded transparency. They demanded appeals. They demanded systems that could explain themselves. And when they did not get what they wanted, they organized.

One young woman named Talia became their voice. After being denied entry to a prestigious university by an opaque admissions AI, she began investigating how the system worked. What she found was familiar: historical data that favored elite schools, wealthy families, and certain cultural backgrounds. The future was being decided by the past.

Talia and her peers used technology to fight technology. They built tools to analyze AI decisions, expose bias, and share stories of injustice. Millions joined. Governments listened. Companies changed.

Slowly, systems began to open up. Scores were explained. Data was questioned. Humans regained a measure of control.

The Unscored were not anti-technology. They were pro-human. And in a world run by machines, that made all the difference.

Chapter 12

Rebuilding Trust in Algorithmic Systems

Trust is the invisible infrastructure of every functioning society. It allows people to cooperate, to accept decisions they do not like, and to believe that institutions are acting in good faith. As artificial intelligence increasingly makes decisions that affect employment, credit, healthcare, safety, and freedom, trust in algorithms has become just as important as trust in human institutions. Without it, even the most accurate systems will be rejected, resisted, or ignored. Rebuilding trust in algorithmic systems is therefore one of the greatest challenges and opportunities of the AI era.

Trust in AI has been damaged by years of opaque, biased, and poorly governed deployments. People have seen algorithms deny loans without explanation, misidentify faces, exclude qualified job candidates, and misjudge medical risk. Each of these failures chips away at public confidence. When individuals feel powerless in the face of automated decisions, they begin to view technology as an enemy rather than a tool. Restoring trust requires more than technical fixes—it requires a cultural shift in how AI is designed, deployed, and governed.

One of the most important elements of trust is transparency. People must be able to understand how decisions are made and what data is used. This does not mean exposing every line of code, but it does mean providing meaningful explanations. A person denied a loan or a job deserves to know why. An AI system that cannot provide reasons undermines its own legitimacy. Explainability transforms algorithms from mysterious oracles into accountable partners.

Accountability is equally essential. Trust cannot exist without responsibility. Organizations that deploy AI must be willing to take responsibility for its outcomes, even when those outcomes are produced by complex models. This means having clear lines of ownership, governance structures, and escalation paths. When something goes wrong, there must be someone who can be held to account and who has the authority to fix it.

Fairness is another cornerstone of trust. People will tolerate mistakes if they believe the system is trying to be just. They will not tolerate a system that consistently favors some groups over others. This is why bias testing, fairness metrics, and audits are so important. They provide evidence that an organization is actively working to treat people equitably.

Participation also builds trust. When communities affected by AI have a voice in how it is used, they are more likely to accept it. This can include public consultations, stakeholder panels, and feedback mechanisms. AI should not be imposed on people. It should be developed with them.

Finally, trust grows through consistency and humility. Organizations must be willing to admit mistakes, learn from them, and improve. AI systems will never be perfect, but they can become better over time if they are guided by a commitment to ethical responsibility.

Rebuilding trust in algorithmic systems is not a technical project—it is a social one. It requires aligning technology with human values. When people believe that AI is working for them rather than against them, the full potential of intelligent systems can finally be realized.

"The Day the Machines Apologized"

No one had expected an apology.

For years, the city's AI systems had made decisions that felt cold and distant. People were denied housing, rejected from schools, and flagged by security algorithms without ever knowing why. Complaints went unanswered. Appeals disappeared into digital voids. Trust in the city's technology collapsed.

Then one morning, every resident received a message.

The city announced that its AI systems would begin issuing explanations and, when appropriate, apologies. If a system made a mistake, it would say so. If a person was harmed, the system would acknowledge it and trigger a human review.

At first, people were skeptical. But then the letters started to arrive.

Maria received one explaining why her housing application had been delayed. The system had used outdated data. It apologized and corrected the error. Jamal received one explaining why his business loan had been denied. The model had misclassified his income. A human officer reviewed it and approved the loan.

These were small things, but they mattered.

Slowly, the city began to change. People started to believe that the machines were no longer untouchable. They were part of a system that could listen, learn, and make amends.

Trust did not return overnight. But it returned.

And for the first time, the algorithms felt a little more human—and a lot more just.

Final Thoughts

Artificial intelligence has now reached a point where it quietly shapes the destiny of billions of people. It decides who gets hired, who gets a loan, who receives healthcare, who is investigated by police, and who is granted opportunity. Yet most people never see these decisions being made. They experience only the result: an approval, a denial, a ranking, or a silent exclusion. This invisibility makes algorithmic bias one of the most dangerous forces of the modern era. When injustice is automated, it becomes harder to detect, harder to fight, and far more powerful than any single human discriminator ever could be.

Throughout this book, we have seen that bias in AI is not accidental. It emerges from data that reflects historical inequality, from models that optimize the wrong objectives, from organizations that fail to test outcomes, and from systems that are deployed without accountability. Every unfair outcome has a technical cause, a business decision, and a governance failure behind it. This means bias is not inevitable. It is engineered. And what is engineered can be redesigned.

The future of AI will be decided not by algorithms alone, but by the standards we demand of them. Societies that allow biased AI to operate without oversight will experience digital forms of segregation, financial exclusion, and systemic injustice. Societies that demand transparency, fairness, and accountability will harness

AI as a tool for opportunity, inclusion, and social progress. This is not a distant future. It is happening now.

Fair AI is not a fantasy. It is a discipline. It requires fairness metrics, audits, governance, ethical design, and legal accountability. It requires companies to treat algorithms as regulated decision-makers, not as magic boxes. It requires engineers to think about people, not just performance. And it requires leaders to accept responsibility for the machines they unleash into the world.

Most importantly, it requires courage. Courage to measure uncomfortable truths. Courage to correct profitable but unjust systems. Courage to choose long-term trust over short-term gain. The organizations that embrace these principles will become the trusted stewards of the AI era. Those that ignore them will face public backlash, legal action, and reputational collapse.

Bias is not the enemy of innovation. It is the enemy of legitimacy. And in the age of AI, legitimacy is everything.

This book is not just about protecting people from harm. It is about building systems that deserve to be used. AI that is fair is AI that lasts.

www.ingramcontent.com/pod-product-compliance
Lightning Source LLC
LaVergne TN
LVHW022026200926
848481LV00007B/2560
* 9 7 9 8 2 9 5 5 3 3 1 3 6 *